FRANCIS FRITH'S
TOWN & CITY
MEMORIES

CONGLETON

ALAN CHRISTOPHER BRADLEY is a retired engineer who has lived
in Congleton since 1968. He has been interested for many years in
local, industrial and family history and is a member of Congleton
History Society, Congleton Museum Trust, the Family History Society
of Cheshire, the Etruria Volunteer Working Party and the Midland Mills
Group. He served for ten years on the committee of Congleton History
Society and edited the first ten issues of its Journal. He now looks
after the collection of photographs at Congleton Museum.
Chris has written (as Alan Bradley) several books on computer subjects
and two books of short walks in the Peak District, and has also written
articles on local industries and on local and family history.

CONGLETON MUSEUM
A museum illustrating the history of Congleton was opened in 2002.
With the aid of exhibits, tableaux, models and computer displays this
tells the story of the town from prehistoric times to the present day.
The Museum library holds a collection of photographs and maps,
besides books on the town and the county. Many of the photographs
can be seen on the Museum's web site. The Museum is located in
Market Square, behind the Town Hall, and is open from 12 to 4.30 on
Tuesday to Friday and Sunday, and 10 to 4.30 on Saturday.
There is a small admission charge.
Telephone: 01260 276360
email: info@congletonmuseum.co.uk
website: www.congletonmuseum.co.uk

CONGLETON, DUKE STREET c1955 C151037

FRANCIS FRITH'S

TOWN&CITY

MEMORIES

CONGLETON

ALAN CHRISTOPHER BRADLEY

FRANCIS FRITH'S
TOWN & CITY
MEMORIES

First published as Congleton, A Photographic History of your Town
in 2001 by Black Horse Books, an imprint of The Francis Frith Collection®
Revised paperback edition published in the United Kingdom in 2005 by
The Francis Frith Collection as Congleton, Town and City Memories

Limited hardback edition ISBN 1-84589-046-9

Paperback edition 2005 ISBN 1-85937-977-X

British Library Cataloguing in Publication Data

Congleton
Town and City Memories
Alan Christopher Bradley

The Francis Frith Collection®
Frith's Barn, Teffont,
Salisbury, Wiltshire SP3 5QP
Tel: +44 (0) 1722 716 376
Email: info@francisfrith.co.uk
www.francisfrith.co.uk

Aerial photographs reproduced under licence from Simmons Aerofilms Limited
Historical Ordnance Survey maps reproduced under licence from Homecheck.co.uk

Printed and bound in England

Front Cover: **CONGLETON**, Lawton Street 1898 42154t
The colour-tinting in this image is for illustrative purposes only,
and is not intended to be historically accurate

FRANCIS FRITH'S
TOWN & CITY
MEMORIES

CONTENTS

THE MAKING OF AN ARCHIVE

Francis Frith, Victorian founder of the world-famous photographic archive, was a devout Quaker and a highly successful Victorian businessman. By 1860 he was already a multi-millionaire, having established and sold a wholesale grocery business in Liverpool. He had also made a series of pioneering photographic journeys to the Nile region. The images he returned with were the talk of London. An eminent modern historian has likened their impact on the population of the time to that on our own generation of the first photographs taken on the surface of the moon.

Frith had a passion for landscape, and was as equally inspired by the countryside of Britain as he was by the desert regions of the Nile. He resolved to set out on a new career and to use his skills with a camera. He established a business in Reigate as a specialist publisher of topographical photographs.

Frith lived in an era of immense and sometimes violent change. For the poor in the early part of Victoria's reign work was a drudge and the hours long, and ordinary people had precious little free time. Most had not travelled far beyond the boundaries of their own town or village. Mass tourism was in its infancy during the 1860s, but during the next decade the railway network and the establishment of Bank Holidays and half-Saturdays gradually made it possible for the working man and his family to enjoy holidays and to see a little more of the world. With characteristic business acumen, Francis Frith foresaw that these new tourists would enjoy having souvenirs to commemorate their days out. He began selling photo-souvenirs of seaside resorts and beauty spots, which the Victorian public pasted into treasured family albums.

Frith's aim was to photograph every town and village in Britain. For the next thirty years he travelled the country by train and by pony and trap, producing fine photographs of seaside resorts and beauty spots that were keenly bought by millions of Victorians.

THE RISE OF FRITH & CO

Each photograph was taken with tourism in mind, the small team of Frith photographers concentrating on busy shopping streets, beaches, seafronts, picturesque lanes and villages. They also photographed buildings: the Victorian and Edwardian eras were times of huge building activity, and town halls, libraries, post offices, schools and technical colleges were springing up all over the country. They were invariably celebrated by a proud Victorian public, and photo souvenirs – visual records – published by F Frith & Co were sold in their hundreds of thousands. In addition, many new commercial buildings such as hotels, inns and pubs were photographed, often because their owners specifically commissioned Frith postcards or prints of them for re-sale or for publicity purposes.

In order to gain some understanding of the scale of Frith's business one only has to look at the catalogue issued by Frith & Co in 1886: it runs to some 670 pages. By 1890 Frith had created the greatest specialist photographic publishing company in the world, with over 2,000 stockists! The picture on the right shows the Frith & Co display board on the wall of the stockist at Ingleton in the Yorkshire Dales (left of window). Beautifully constructed with a mahogany frame and gilt inserts, it displayed a dozen scenes.

POSTCARD BONANZA

The ever-popular holiday postcard we know today took many years to appear, and F Frith & Co was in the vanguard of its development. Postcards became a hugely popular means of communication and sold in their millions. Frith's company took full advantage of this boom and soon became the major publisher of photographic view postcards.

Francis Frith died in 1898 at his villa in Cannes, his great project still growing. His sons Eustace and Cyril continued their father's monumental task, expanding the number of views offered to the public and recording more and more places in Britain, as the coasts and countryside were opened up to mass travel. The archive Frith created continued in business for another seventy years. By 1970 it contained over a third of a million pictures of 7,000 cities, towns and villages. The massive photographic record Frith has left to us stands as a living monument to a special and very remarkable man.

This book shows your town as it was photographed by this world-famous archive at various periods in its development over the past 150 years. Every photograph was taken for a specific commercial purpose, which explains why the selection may not show every aspect of the town landscape. However, the photographs, compiled from one of the world's most celebrated archives, provide an important and absorbing record of your town.

FROM THE AIR

CONGLETON FROM THE AIR 1929 AF28121

LAWTON STREET 1898 42154

INTRODUCTION

Photograph 42154 (pages 10-11) is perhaps the finest of the Frith photographs of Congleton, with every detail pin-sharp. It shows the main street of the town, looking westwards.

In the foreground the road is called Lawton Street, but at the dip it changes its name to High Street. The tower of the Town Hall is prominent to the right; while the house on the left, with the curved steps, is Bradshaw House, which stands on the site of the home of John Bradshaw, attorney and one-time Mayor of Congleton. John Bradshaw later moved to London to become head of the royal court which condemned Charles I to death. The house opposite, with its gable end on the street, is obviously timber-framed, as the upper storey juts out over the lower portion of the house. However, like many similar buildings, it has been plastered over to protect the timber.

Horse transport is much in evidence, as is its by-product, horse manure. An account book which survives from a slightly earlier period records the 'Rental for the sweeping of the streets'; evidently people were prepared to pay the council for the privilege of collecting horse manure, which they presumably sold to local gardeners. The second cart, to the left of the photograph, appears to be carrying milk churns and was probably making doorstep deliveries. The milk was ladled from the churn with a pint or half-pint measure, and poured straight into the purchaser's own jug.

Compare this picture with the similar view from the 1950s, C151034 (pages 14-15).

Congleton has a long, if uneventful, history. Some finds of prehistoric material indicate that early man passed this way, but there is no evidence that he settled here. Anglo-Saxons are known to have lived at Davenport, a few miles downstream, and that was probably the origin of our town. The first mention of Congleton is in the Domesday Book (compiled in 1086), where it is described as a small farming settlement. By 1272, when Congleton was granted its first charter, it had become a market town.

Congleton suffered, like other towns, from plagues, floods and civil wars. However, the most significant event in its later history came in the 1750s, when a water-powered silk mill was built on the river bank. This was only the fourth such mill in the country, and at the time it was the largest. It was 240ft long, 48ft high, but only 24ft wide, in order to make the best use of daylight.

The mill was built to house a number of machines for 'throwing' silk; that is, for preparing the unwound filaments from silkworm cocoons, and combining and twisting them into a strong thread. The machinery was driven by a single waterwheel. This wheel, and the other machinery, was designed by the famous millwright and engineer James Brindley, who was in business as a millwright in Leek about this time. The waterwheel was powered by water flowing over a weir, which was originally built to supply the town's corn mill; however, the proprietors

THE OLD MILL 1902 48675

of the silk mill bought the corn mill to secure the water rights. It continued to operate until the 1960s when it was demolished as unsafe. The waterwheel of the silk mill was eventually supplemented by one of the first steam engines in Cheshire. All the old machinery is now gone, and when the mill itself became unsafe in the 1930s it was reduced to two storeys. It was demolished in 2002, and has been replaced by housing. After the demolition, archaeologists excavated the water wheel pit and the foundations of the steam engine house.

The original silk mill became known as the 'Old Mill' as others were built around the town. At a stroke, these mills turned Congleton from a quiet market town with high unemployment into one of the UK's first industrial towns. Thereafter, industry developed extensively in the town, mainly in the various branches of the textile trade, until the 20th century, when new industries were introduced and textiles declined. The town corn mill can be seen at the right of the picture.

THE TOWN CENTRE

THE TOWN HALL AND HIGH STREET C1955 C151034

This photograph is taken from a point slightly nearer the centre than 42154 on pages 10-11. The foreground is still Lawton Street but High Street begins at the junction in front of the timber framed building on the right. The old gas lamp-post on the left, now without its lantern, is the one seen behind the nearest horse in the older picture.

Congleton continued - and continues - to serve as a market town, though it is commercially somewhat overshadowed by its larger neighbour, Macclesfield. The layout of the main street and its offshoots is said to have changed little since medieval times. The main street changes its name, as one travels westwards, from Lawton Street to High Street, then to Bridge Street and eventually Duke Street. It then forms a T-junction with another old street, which begins as Swan Bank before changing its name to Mill Street. Little Street, with its timber-framed cottages, and Colehill Bank, are other ancient streets, although Market Street is more recent. Dog Lane, another very old road, was renamed Canal Street when the canal wharf opened alongside it, nearly a mile from the town centre. The buildings in all these streets are of modest height, with only the 19th century Town Hall towering above them.

In C151034 (opposite) the horses and carts have been replaced by cars and lorries - at this time, and in fact until the 1980s, the main road from Chester to Buxton ran through the town centre. The traditional gas lamp-posts have been replaced by ugly concrete ones, after electricity finally reached Congleton in 1931. The row of houses behind the horses in the earlier picture - cottages bordering Water Street, which no longer exists - has been demolished and replaced by a small garden containing the War Memorial which is hidden behind the wall with the circus poster on the left of C151034 and by the Premier Cinema which today has been replaced by a peaceful 'community garden'. The timbered building on the right is the King's Arms, which features in a later photograph in this book.

Otherwise, apart from the shop fronts and signs, little has changed since 1898 and indeed the scene looks much the same today.

In photograph 42155 (page 16) we have passed the Town Hall and are looking back at it. The picture is dated 1898, but could be any date up to the present day, except for the shop fronts and the iron gates closing the arches of the Town Hall. Of these only the central pair, giving access to the interior of the hall remain today, but the open arcades on either side (the one on the left once housed part of the market) have since been enclosed.

The timber-framed shop on the left, with its jutting upper stories, is one of the oldest buildings in Congleton: at one time it had a small bellcote on the gable end. Today it is Davenport's, the gentlemen's outfitters. It was evidently a grocer and general store, the type of shop that could be found by the dozen in the average high street, until they were wiped out by the spread of the

THE TOWN CENTRE

in most towns, very few original shop fronts remain from the 19th century, although above the facias several buildings in the main street are little changed. In Frith's day most of the shops were locally owned; now the majority are branches of national chains. Grocers' shops, the mainstay of the day's shopping in Frith's time, have long gone from the town centre, to be replaced by building societies, travel agents, and betting shops.

Turning westward again (49476, page 20-21), the photographer was standing in the road outside the Town Hall. Horses and carts are again in evidence. Most of the buildings shown in this picture still exist, although the Black Boy Inn, with its overhanging roof, beyond the lamp-post on the right, has gone; also, a couple of the old shops on the left have been replaced by a modern building.

The timbered building to the left of the picture is the White Lion, one of the oldest inns in Congleton; at one time its frontage was wider, but it was partly replaced by the brick building just beyond it. The sign of its close neighbour, the Black Lion, can be seen on the extreme left. Entry to this pub was via a narrow alleyway, now a private yard, whose entrance can just be seen below the gas lamp.

In C151038 (page 22) we see how little the town has changed in 50-odd years except for the shop fronts and the street furniture - and of course the clothes of the passers-by. The bus in the distance appears to be parked on a small patch of open ground which today is occupied by a flower bed. Twenty years later, with the increase in traffic, it would have been dangerous to walk in the road. Today the High Street is no longer a main traffic route, though dodging between parked cars can still be hazardous.

Close inspection shows that the Chronicle Office, the building on the right with the round-headed Venetian window, has been truncated - in the earlier picture there were two such windows - and partly replaced by the Trustee Savings Bank. The projecting canopy of the Capitol Cinema can be seen in the middle of the picture. This cinema

supermarket. Loaves are stacked by the door and what appears to be a side of bacon hangs above. The shop boy sweeps the pavement, while his opposite number at the next shop struggles with a canvas canopy. Children stand idly around - no television for them to watch!

The photo opposite, on page 17, shows the same scene nearly 60 years later. The shops have changed hands, but otherwise only the bicycles and the road markings reveal the passage of time. As

succumbed to competition from TV in the 1960s and has since been replaced by an arcade of small shops.

Davenport's is on the extreme right, and the chemist's shop next door remained in business, with a succession of proprietors, until very recently.

Moving westwards again, we come at last to the end of the main street (C151037, pages 26-27), with yet another change of name. At the end of Little Street, which runs off to the left by the first lamp-post, Bridge Street becomes Duke Street (formerly Duck Street) - although quite a few Congleton people are unaware of this fact.

The road running past the end of Duke Street also changes its name; it is Swan Bank to the left, and Mill Street to the right. To the left of it, just by the lamp-post, one can see the ornate building, complete with turret, occupied by the District Bank, which after several mergers and name changes closed in the 1990s. It is now a pub, 'The Counting House'.

The sharp bend from Mill Street into Duke Street caused serious traffic problems when longer commercial vehicles became common. From time to time, they became stuck at this point - a situation that was not solved until Mountbatten Way opened, taking all the traffic away.

The timber-framed building on the right of C151037 has since been replaced by modern shops, as has the building opposite, just beyond the end of Little Street.

LEFT: THE TOWN HALL 1898 42155

ABOVE: THE TOWN HALL C1965 C151078

Spot the difference! Apart from the shop fronts, the only change is the bus stop marked out on road on the right and the bicycles - popular before heavy traffic made cycling in the town centre a hazardous pursuit.

This is a closer view of the Town Hall and the adjoining shops, with an unusual absence of traffic. The shop on the right still retains the glass canopy shown here.

HIGH STREET 1903 49476

HIGH STREET C1955
C151038

THE TOWN CENTRE

BRIDGE STREET C1955 C151035

The main street changes its name from High Street to Bridge Street just beyond the place where the photographer was standing. At its lowest point, the street bridges the Howty Brook, although because the brook passes through a culvert beneath the shops on either side, it cannot be seen. Road traffic is apparent, but as it is mostly parked vans and lorries, the street must still have been reasonably quiet. It is a pedestrian precinct today, and the concrete lamp-posts have been replaced by more attractive street furniture with flowerbeds and trees. Most of the buildings on the left survive today, although the ones in the foreground on the right have been rebuilt further back from the main thoroughfare. Woolworths, seen on the right, has now moved next door to replace the Bear's Head Inn, just out of sight to the right of this picture. W H Smiths has taken its place.

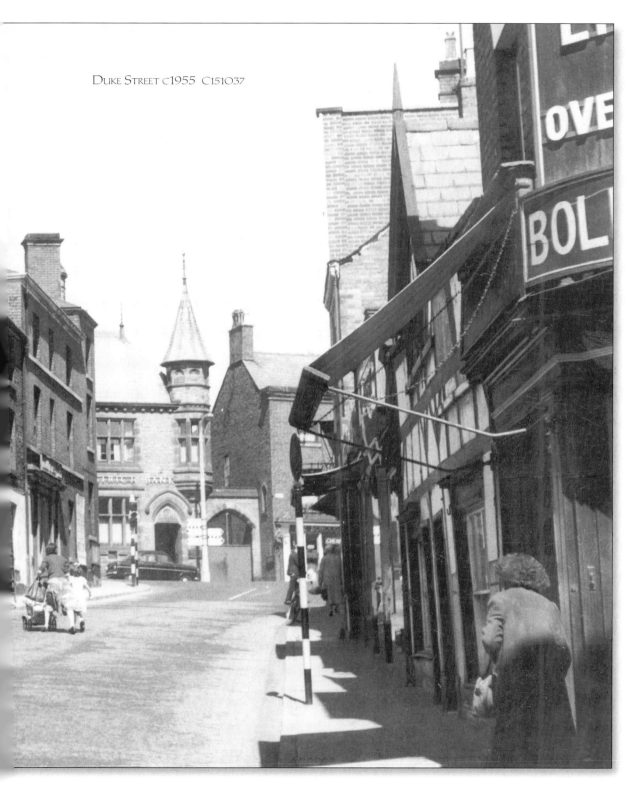

DUKE STREET c1955 C151037

THE CHURCHES

ABOVE ST PETER'S CHURCH 1898 42157

Taken from the west, this picture shows the stone tower and the brick body of the church, with its industrial-looking cast iron window frames.

RIGHT: ST PETER'S CHURCH, THE INTERIOR 1898 42159

The photographer was looking eastwards from the entrance. At this time, all but the uppermost section of the east window had clear glass. Stained glass was introduced later in 1922. Although not discernible in this picture (perhaps because of the glare from the windows), there are two oil paintings by Edward Penny on either side of the window, which were painted in 1748. They depict St Paul and St Peter.

Congleton has several churches, but only one pre-dates the 19th century. This is St Peter's, which was largely rebuilt in the 18th century. The Catholic church, St Mary's, dates from 1826; and the remaining churches and chapels were built from 1840 or later.

St Peter's is close to the town centre but is hidden from the main street. Until 1868, when it acquired its own parish, it was technically a 'chapel of ease', a subsidiary to the mother church of Astbury in whose parish it lay. This explains why the street that passes the church is called Chapel Street. In practice, the church was under the control of the municipal authorities, and attempts by successive rectors of Astbury to assert their control over it seem to have met with little success.

The date the first church was built on this site is unknown, but in 1404 it was rebuilt or replaced by a timber-framed nave with a stone chancel and tower. As the town's population increased this became too small, and in 1740 the church was demolished, apart from the lower stages of the tower. It was replaced by the present day building, which seats over a thousand. Frith photographs show the church at various times between 1898 and 1960. However, there are no discernible differences between them, other than the tarmacing of the setts and expanded tree canopies. Apart from the parked cars, the scene is much the same today.

Although plain outside, the church has a fine Georgian interior. Broad galleries occupy three sides, and at the east end behind the altar is an impressive wooden reredos with a Venetian three-light window above.

The unusual central pulpit was taken from Astbury church in the 1870s, replacing a three-decker pulpit that stood in the same position. It was removed during the 1970s and replaced by a simple reading desk. Otherwise the church has changed little since 1898, and the uncomfortable box pews remain. The front pew, to the right of the church, was reserved for the Mayor and his party. It is just possible to make out in photograph 42159 (page 21) the rampant lion in gilded wood at the nearest corner of the second pillar on the right. It served as a holder for the Mayor's symbol of authority, the town mace, and is still there today.

In C151060 (page 31) the photographer was facing west from the reading desk that stood in front of the central pulpit. The organ can be seen in the west gallery, and in front of it the magnificent brass chandelier holding sixteen candles, which dates from 1748. The glazed inner doors are probably the only new feature since 1898 (apart from the electric light fitting behind the chandelier). The doors were made by a local craftsman, Sam Frodsham, who carried out extensive work here and in other local churches.

Some of the many memorial tablets on the walls and pillars are visible in this picture. A church guidebook from about 1930 considers that these 'do not enhance the beauty' of the interior, although they are much improved as the result of recent cleaning. Some are of considerable historical interest.

THE CHURCHES

ST STEPHEN'S CHURCH 1898 42161

St Stephen's is typical of its period, built during a revival of the Early English style. Funds did not run to a tower. It stands today very much as the photographer saw it in 1898.

Until the mid 19th century the entire town of Congleton lay in the large parish of Astbury, although, as we have seen, the 'chapel of ease' of St Peter's served the people of the town. However, as the population of England grew, the government provided money for an ambitious building programme. New churches were built in and around the town, and parishes assigned to them: the church of St James, west of the town centre; St Stephen, to the north-east; and Holy Trinity, further out to the south-east. All of these date from this period, as does St John's Church at Buglawton. Today all these churches, except St James's, have joined with St Peter's to form the Congleton Team Parish.

Like many Northern towns, Congleton had several Nonconformist places of worship by the end of the 19th century. The Congregational Church was built in 1876 and stands in Antrobus Street, a short distance from the town centre (42160, pages 36-37). It has been built in the popular Gothic style, and has double doorways and a short corner tower with a spire. It looks much the same today, except that the spire has gone, leaving the tower with a flat roof bearing a metal cross. It is now known as the United Reform Church.

ABOVE: ST PETER'S CHURCH,
THE INTERIOR C1960 C151059

This shows in more detail the carved wood-
en reredos, or ornamental screen behind
the altar, with its biblical texts. Just visible
at each side of the window are the edges
of the two paintings of apostles, which are
not quite visible in the picture 42159, on
page 29.

RIGHT: ST PETER'S CHURCH,
THE INTERIOR C1960 C151060

CONGLETON

ST JOHN'S CHURCH, BUGLAWTON 1898 42170

Buglawton, though very close to Congleton, was independent until the 1930s. This church was built in 1840, and paid for mainly by voluntary subscriptions. It is oriented north-south, so that the front faces the road. Its style is generally Norman in character, unusual for the period. Once again, little has changed today.

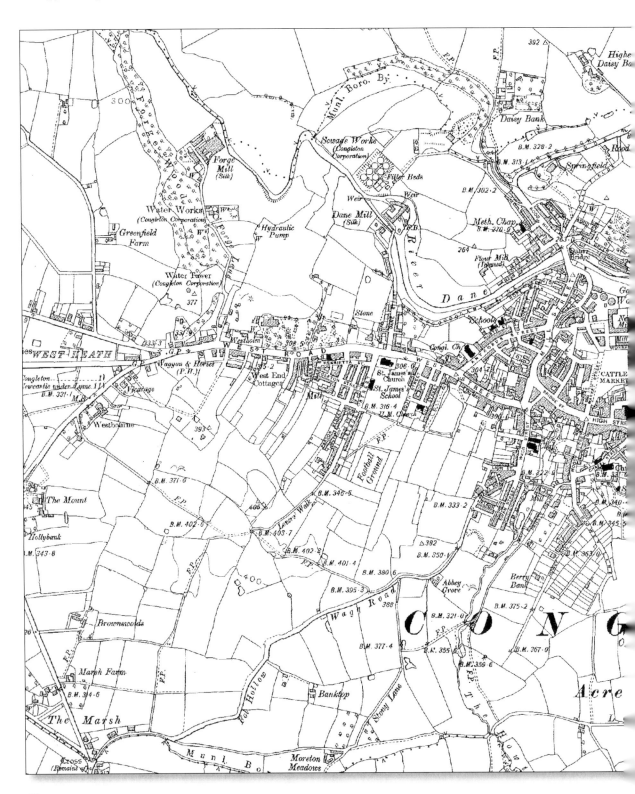

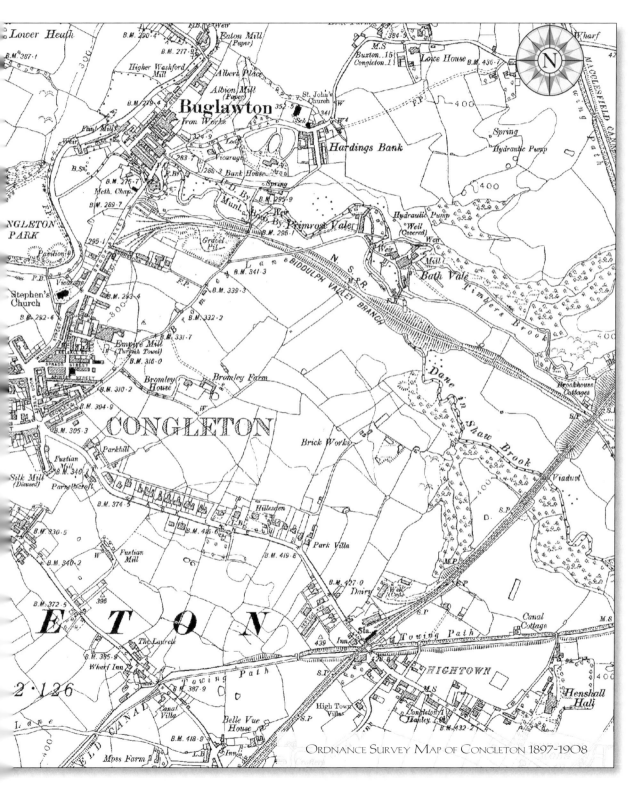

ORDNANCE SURVEY MAP OF CONGLETON 1897-1908

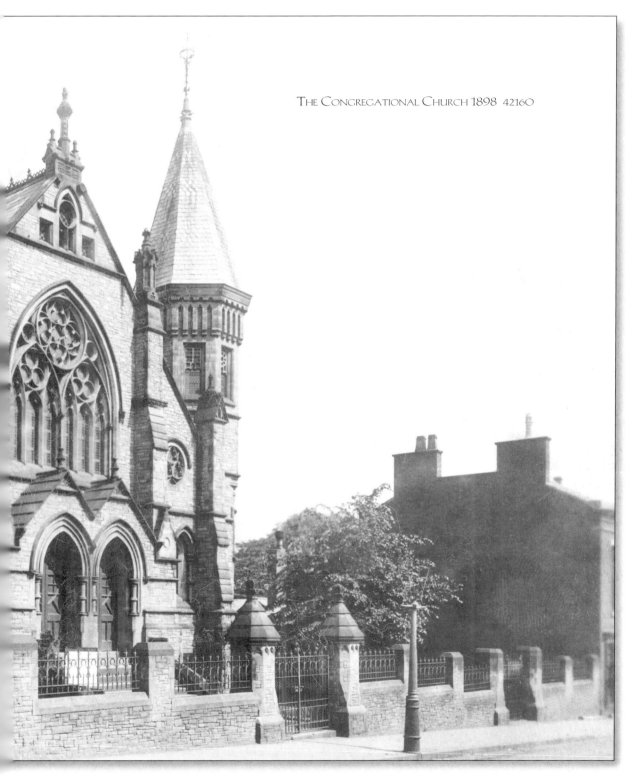

The Congregational Church 1898 42160

OLD PUBS AND HOUSES

In its early days Congleton must have been in the main a town of timber-framed buildings, though there is mention of a 'stone hall' in one 1404 document. Now it is mostly brick, but a few timber-framed buildings remain. Prominent among these is the White Lion pub opposite the Town Hall.

The King's Arms, a few steps to the east, is probably the oldest pub in Congleton and is thought to date back to 1585, although it had a different name at that time. It stands on the corner of Kinsey Street at the point where the main street becomes known as High Street (C151036, pages 40-41), and can also be seen in some of the earlier photographs in this book. The entire frontage is timber-framed, apart from the single-storey extension beyond the gable. Since this photograph was taken, all the timbering has been exposed and restored.

The Lion and Swan Hotel is the largest of

Congleton's old inns. It existed, under the name of The Swan, as early as 1651. Four coaches stopped here daily at the beginning of the 19th century. The front of the building appears to be timber-framed, but only the middle part, including the porch and the room above it, is original. The wings, together with the single storey projection left of the porch, are 19th century - you can just see that the left wall is built of brick over a stone base.

Later photographs from the 1950s show no change to the building apart from the addition of a hanging sign at the front, and the replacement of the gas lamp-post with an electric, concrete one. This scene looks practically the same today.

Smaller timber-framed buildings can be seen in Lawton Street, Moody Street and Little Street. Others exist but are hidden by later frontages. A few more survive in the surrounding countryside, and a couple of miles along the Manchester Road is the timber-framed Marton Church, one of the earliest and most complete examples in the country.

THE KING'S ARMS
C1965 C151036

THE MARKET AND THE PARK

The town still has its market, authorised by the charter of 1272, although it has been moved a number of times. There is no ancient market place, and its original location in High Street must have disrupted the traffic. From there it moved to Market Square behind the Town Hall, and then later to an open space known as the 'fairground', or more familiarly the 'tip' - these being its two main functions. Today the old fairground is occupied by the library, the bus station and a car park, although once or twice a year a funfair is somehow squeezed in. Meanwhile the market has a new home beside a supermarket, hidden away from the main streets.

The town's market cross has had a troubled history. There seems to have been a cross in High Street, the site of the old weekly market, as early as 1500. It was replaced in 1707 by another cross, which was removed in 1772, 'being considered a nuisance', presumably because it obstructed the traffic. Thereafter it disappeared, but some fragments - possibly not all from the same cross - were preserved. In 1902, to celebrate the coronation of Edward the Sixth, the pieces were reassembled with some newly made sections, and the structure placed in a small garden to form the cross seen in photograph 48674 (pages 44-45). Later the cross was removed from this site to make room for the War Memorial, and what is left of it now stands in the park.

Congleton Park, across the river from the town centre, was opened in 1871 and has been popular ever since. Vandalism and maintenance costs had reduced its amenities, but a lottery grant recently financed a scheme of refurbishment. The local authority maintains a display of flowers in the park and elsewhere in the town, on a scale that puts many larger boroughs to shame. The council also supports amateurs who make a brave show of 'Congleton in Bloom' each year.

Near the park entrance today, there are some curious decorated stone pinnacles which were probably garden ornaments, though their exact origin appears to have been forgotten. At the far corner of the park is a structure on which, for many years, stood a gun captured during the Crimean War; but this fell victim to a government campaign to collect scrap metal for the war effort around 1940. An ornate Victorian horse trough and drinking fountain, which once stood near the town bridge, was moved to the park in the 1970s, after being knocked down once too often by passing vehicles.

CONGLETON PARK C1955 C151022

Frith photographers always made a point of recording local parks, and there are no fewer than fourteen pictures of Congleton Park. This picture, taken near the park entrance, shows the market cross in its new home.

THE MARKET AND THE PARK

RIGHT: THE MARKET CROSS 1902 48674

Here is the old cross after its restoration. The location is the plot where the war memorial now stands, near the east end of the High Street with Cole Hill Bank behind it.

BELOW: CONGLETON PARK C1950 C151007

This view of the park is included here to show how prominent the hill named The Cloud is, visible from even the lower areas of Congleton.

LEFT: DETAIL FROM C151007

The Jubilee Pavilion, near the park entrance, was built to celebrate Queen Victoria's diamond jubilee: it was damaged by fire in the 1990s but has now been renovated and extended.

A popular feature of the park at one time was a small fleet of rowing boats. They plied a short length of river, just 200 or 300 yards between two weirs. They appear in each batch of Frith's photographs, but are no longer there today.

At the back of Congleton Park a steep bank rises from the level flood plain of the river to the plateau above (48677, page 55). This bank is covered with trees which represent the last remnants of the town wood, "a league long and a league broad", which was mentioned in Domesday book. No doubt several generations of trees have come and gone since then. The Victorian creators of the park incorporated this wood in their design, and built a network of paths. The wood is carpeted with bluebells in the spring.

CONGLETON PARK C1960 C151046

Taken only a few years after photograph C151022 (pages 42-43) this corner of the park has been transformed. The cross has been moved back and a broad path, with central flower beds, leads up to it, with more flowerbeds on either side. Today, after damage by vandals, the new head and tall shaft of the cross have been removed; only two older sections and the plinth remain. A spectacular display of flowers is still maintained.

THE MARKET AND THE PARK

CONGLETON PARK, THE RIVER DANE 1898 42163

This view was taken looking downstream. The Jubilee Pavilion (celebrating Queen Victoria's diamond jubilee) can be seen through the trees. The chimney in the background belongs to the Old Mill. Nowadays the chimney and the boats have gone, along with the arched shelter behind the boats.

CONGLETON PARK AND THE RIVER DANE C1960 C151063

This photograph was taken from the bridge seen in the previous picture (42163, page 48), this time looking upstream with the park on the left and Hankinson's Field on the right. The second park bridge can be seen in the centre, and St Stephen's church is just behind the trees on the right. There are still boats, although they look shorter and tubbier than the ones of 60 years earlier.

THE MARKET AND THE PARK

ABOVE: CONGLETON PARK C1955 C151039

In another corner of the park is a bowling green with its own timber pavilion. It is still in regular use today.

PARK WOODS 1902 48677

CONGLETON PARK,
THE JUBILEE PAVILION
1898 42165

This offers a closer look at
the pavilion shown in an
earlier picture. It was damaged by fire in the 1990s but
has now been restored and
extended.

ROUND AND ABOUT THE TOWN

C ongleton commemorated the dead of the 1914-18 war not only with a War Memorial in Lawton Street, where an annual Remembrance service is still held, but also with a new hospital in Canal Street, which replaced a much smaller building near the town centre.

The hospital was taken over by the National Health Service in the 1950s and has been considerably extended since, so much so that the buildings in our picture (C151020) are now not readily seen. It is still an important part of the life of the town, although accidents and major emergencies (including maternity services!) are dealt with in the larger hospital in Macclesfield.

Another amenity built between the wars was an outdoor swimming pool, typical of a 1930s 'lido' with its fountain and separate blocks of changing rooms for men and women - one of which is shown in photograph C151006 (page 61). The other matching block is situated to the right of the pool. The River Dane is hidden by the fence, but the Town Wood can be seen in the background.

THE WAR MEMORIAL HOSPITAL C1955 C151020

When Frith's photographers returned to the town in the 1950s and 1960s, they recorded some of the newer developments. One of these was the War Memorial Hospital, erected by public subscription in memory of those who fell in the 1914-18 war.

ROUND AND ABOUT THE TOWN

Although it is a sunny day, it is noticeable that there is no-one in the water! Congleton people must have become even less hardy after the war, because this pool was replaced later by an indoor one on another site. The Daneside Theatre, a modern building replacing one that was lost when Mountbatten Way was built, now stands on the site of the old pool.

State education in Congleton followed the usual pattern. There are several primary schools built at various times, and now two post-war High Schools (secondary schools). For several years in the early 20th century, Congleton had a private secondary school, Victoria College. The school occupied a Victorian mansion, off West Road to the south-west of the town centre. It flourished for a few years but eventually ceased to be a school. After more changes the house, together with others nearby, became 'Danesford', a branch of the National Children's Homes, which accommodated difficult or delinquent children. Danesford eventually closed in the 1990s. Today most of the site is a housing estate. One of the other large houses has since become the Woodlands public house and restaurant.

Congleton has one or two substantial Georgian houses near the town centre, but the Victorian mill-owners preferred to live further

and Swan Bank before making another very sharp turn in front of the Lion and Swan Hotel. Traffic passing so close to the town centre must have been good for business, especially for the three or four coaching inns on the route, but it was hardly suitable for the modern motoring age. In 1956 the Clayton Bypass, named after a civic dignitary, took much of the traffic out of the town centre by means of a new bridge over the river.

East-west traffic, particularly on the Buxton to Chester route, continued through the main shopping street. Not infrequently, long lorries became stranded at the sharp bend from Mill Street into Duke Street and Bridge Street. Eventually, in the 1980s, a new 'inner relief road' - christened Mountbatten Way in the aftermath of the assassination of Lord Mountbatten - was built and much of the main street became a pedestrian area.

Later photographs show a number of roads in and near the town. One interesting collection illustrates how the Clayton Bypass relieved one of the town's worst traffic problems - the bend shown in C151021 (page 60-61). The bypass is pictured in C151064 (page 60) from a point near the roundabout at its southern end. The new bridge over the river can be seen just beyond the white vans, while the northern end of the bypass, beyond which the existing road continues, is visible in the distance, below the semi-detached houses. There are now traffic lights at that junction.

The area has changed considerably since this photograph was taken. There is a new roundabout beyond the bridge, at the point where a vehicle is pictured turning left; and the nursery gardens which occupied the left-hand side of the road behind the trees have been replaced with commercial premises, with an industrial estate behind. The grass verge on the left has been replaced by a widened pavement which now serves cyclists as well as pedestrians, and there are more houses to the right of the road.

Moving away from the town centre, the Frith photographers captured an atmospheric view of the town (48673, page 64) - probably on a Sunday or a holiday in summer, since there is so little smoke. It seems surprising that so few mill chimneys can be seen, although a close and detailed inspection of the original photograph reveals several of them. The 'west fields', now built over, were once the site of one of the medieval open fields, where each farmer owned one or several narrow unfenced strips of land.

out of town. Popular locations were near the railway station, from where businessmen could travel conveniently to Manchester or Stoke or further afield. Perhaps the most impressive of their homes was Henshall Hall, which stood in its own park beside the Biddulph Road, a short way beyond the station (42169, pages 58-59).

Congleton is situated on the main road from Manchester to Newcastle-under-Lyme, which became a turnpike in 1781. But although the sections north and south of the town were positioned almost along a straight line, traffic from Manchester had to negotiate a very sharp bend and a steep downhill slope as it entered Congleton to reach the only bridge. From here the road climbed Mill Street

ROUND AND ABOUT THE TOWN

Congleton lies on the Macclesfield Canal, but as this runs nearly a mile from the town centre, above a steep hill, it has had little effect on the trade of the town. A wharf and warehouse were built, but there are no signs of canal-side mills (such as there are in Macclesfield and Bollington, for example). Commercial traffic was never heavy, and the canal only had a short useful life from its opening in 1831 until the arrival of the railway less than two decades later. However, the canal is now popular with pleasure boats. The towpath, running mainly through open countryside, makes a pleasant route for walkers.

Congleton's first railway was short, and short-lived - a horse-drawn mineral line which brought coal from a colliery near Mow Cop. However the North Staffordshire Railway's line from Stoke to Macclesfield, with connections to Manchester, opened in 1847, and brought great benefits to the town. A horse-drawn omnibus was soon operating a service along the mile from the town centre to the station. Congleton station, with its adjacent level crossing and tall signal box, was impressive. Both station and level crossing were later swept away, to be replaced by modern buildings and an over-bridge, when the railway was electrified in the 1960s. A branch line from Stoke via Biddulph to Brunswick Wharf in Congleton was used mainly for mineral traffic and workmen's trains. It closed in the 1960s and has become a pleasant footpath.

Just outside Congleton, and now adjoining its suburbs, is Havannah (named after a contemporary military victory in Cuba). It is a fascinating industrial settlement built on a 'green field' site at a point where ample water power was available (see 42172 on page 64). It was established in 1763, when Charles Roe of Macclesfield began copper working. Later, a large silk mill was built. Two streets of terraced cottages were constructed, although many workers must have walked there daily from

Congleton. The fortunes of the local industry ebbed, and at one time the village was virtually deserted. Nowadays, only one of the terraces remains, and the area has become quite popular again. At one time a tobacco company occupied one of the mills, and its products were sold as 'Havannah cigars'!

HENSHALL HALL 1898 42169

This is a typical Victorian mansion, built in brick with stone dressings. This picture shows the mansion's front porch on the left and an imposing conservatory to the right. There is now no trace of the hall - the site and park are now taken over by a modern housing estate.

ROUND AND ABOUT THE TOWN

ABOVE: THE ROUNDABOUT C1960 C151047

This view of the roundabout - a novelty in Congleton - shows where the south end of the bypass joins the existing main road. It looks much the same today, with attractive flower-beds, although it has been reduced in size to aid the flow of the traffic. The house on the right is Mortlake House, which was part of the Danesford Children's Home and is now the Woodlands pub. Many of the trees behind it have been removed to make way for flats and houses. The second building from the left is the Catholic church of St Mary.

BELOW: CLAYTON BYPASS C1960 C151064

ROOD HILL C1950 C151021

Once notoriously dangerous - at one time a 'lighthouse' with an illuminated 'Danger' sign faced descending traffic - this corner had already been improved when this photograph was taken. The bank on the right was excavated to make way for the massive retaining wall that still stands here. At this time, all traffic had to pass over the town bridge, which was situated some way behind the photographer. The new bypass, built shortly after this picture was taken, now leads off to the left, allowing north-south through traffic to continue straight ahead.

THE BATHS C1950 C151006

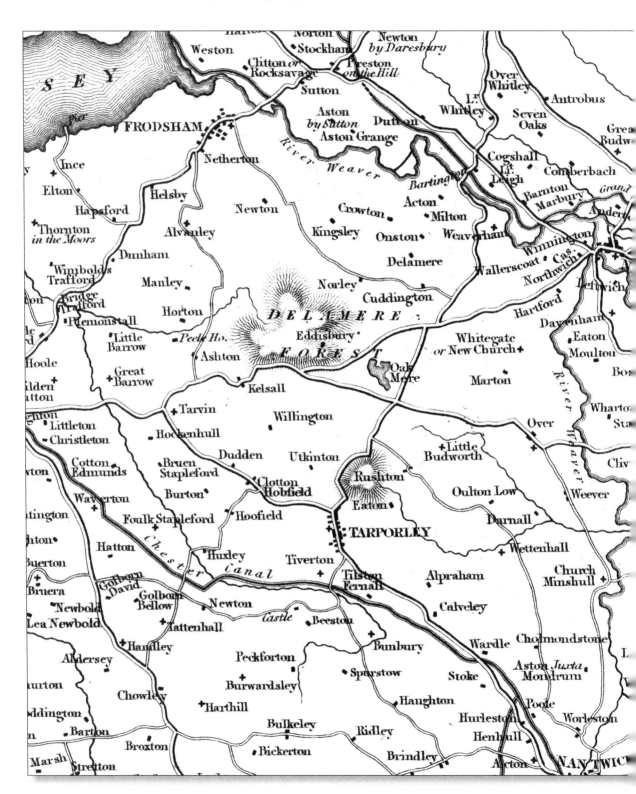

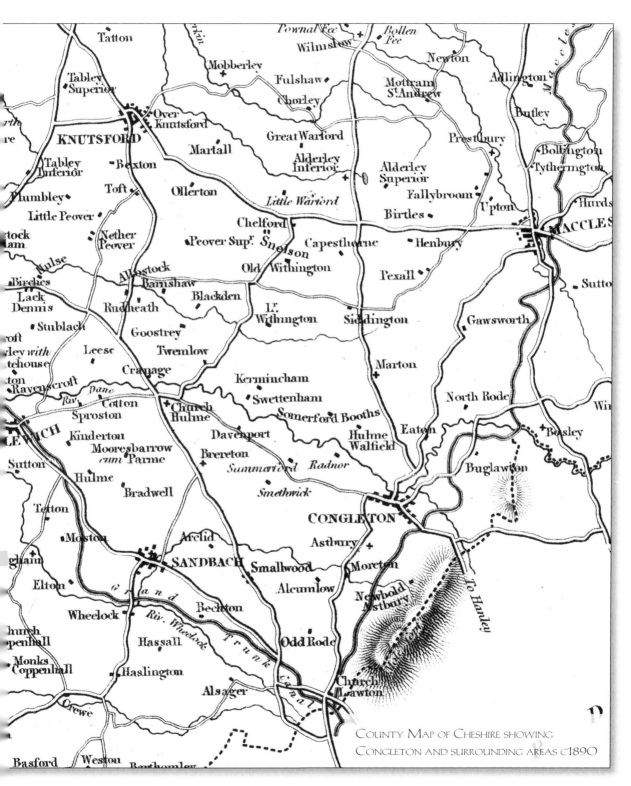

COUNTY MAP OF CHESHIRE SHOWING
CONGLETON AND SURROUNDING AREAS c1890

ROUND AND ABOUT THE TOWN

ABOVE: HAVANNAH, THE WEIR 1898 42172

A view at Havannah showing the massive weir and some of the industrial buildings. These buildings have now disappeared but the weir remains.

BELOW: FROM WEST FIELDS 1902 48673

St Peter's church can be seen just right of centre, with the Town Hall spire visible well to the left.

THE CANAL c1965 C151100

The Macclesfield Canal passes through the outskirts of Congleton, complete with an elegant iron aqueduct where it crosses Canal Street, and several attractive bridges. This view shows some of the locks at Bosley, three miles north-east of the town. Here, twelve locks, spaced out over nearly a mile, raise the canal from the long pound which passes through Congleton to the one which runs through Macclesfield and on to Marple.

HAVANNAH, THE DESERTED VILLAGE 1898 42171

The eight or so people in the photograph probably comprised the entire population.

CONGLETON'S COUNTRYSIDE

Frith's photographers also took pictures of a number of places outside Congleton, and the village of Astbury - just over a mile from the town centre - is perhaps the most significant. Until the 19th century Congleton was part of the large parish of Astbury, although the town had its own church, St Peter's, which was more or less independent.

Astbury has a magnificent church, St Mary's, approached from the village green through a stone archway. The church, a tall building in the Perpendicular style, dominates the little village. The Georgian rectory, the Egerton Arms just across the road and the village green all combine to create a photographer's dream. The church is equally interesting inside although, sadly, it is usually kept locked. It has

a musician's gallery above the west door and an ornate font cover; however the most impressive features are the roofs of the north aisle and of the main church - there is no structural division between nave and chancel. The main roof has a magnificently carved pendant over the chancel.

The countryside surrounding Congleton holds much of interest. Little Moreton Hall (or Moreton Old Hall, as Frith's contemporaries preferred to call it) is an outstanding timber-framed house about four miles to the south-west of Congleton. Parts of the hall date from the 16th century, but its crowning glory is the long gallery above the gatehouse. Shown in photograph 48670 (page 71) reflected in the moat, it has graced the cover of many books. The Hall was given to

This photograph shows
an attractive rural scene
with the impressive church
behind the village green.
The tower, which is older
than the main body of the
church, appears almost
detached from the main
structure at its north-west
corner. What looks like the
stump of a tower at the west
end of the nave is in fact
a three-storey porch. The
village pub and rectory are
just out of sight to the left
of the church. The scene
looks much the same today,
except that the tree is larger.
The green is a mass of daf-
fodils in spring.

the National Trust in the 1930s. Timber framed buildings are usually built with 'green', or unseasoned, oak because it is much easier to work. Often the wood twists as it dries - the spire of Chesterfield Church is the most famous example of such extreme warping - and so timbered buildings are frequently distorted to some extent. Some of the distortion at Little Moreton, however, is due to structural weakness, and the National Trust has recently spent a great deal of money installing hidden steelwork to strengthen the structure. In the fields nearby there are traces of 15th-century iron-working and 18th-century fish farming. The nearby Great Moreton Hall is a vast pile built in 1840 to replace a timber-framed building which, judging by the old pictures, was of a similar period to Little Moreton. Its owner

spent a great deal of money diverting the turnpike road so that it could not be seen from his windows. The two halls take their names from the two townships, Great Moreton and Little Moreton, where they are located.

Little Moreton Hall must be one of the most famous timber-framed buildings in the country. It has always been a favourite with artists and photographers, and in 48670 the Frith photographer has captured it at its most romantic. The massive gatehouse fills the centre of the picture, with the moat in the foreground. The building on the right is the chapel.

The four-square view of the hall, shown in C151031 (page 70), may be less romantic, but it shows the structure of the gatehouse

CONGLETON'S COUNTRYSIDE

TOP: MORETON
OLD HALL C1955
C151031

MIDDLE:
MORETON OLD
HALL, ENTRANCE
C1955 C151013

This close-up picture of the entrance to the gatehouse passage shows some of its fine carving. Reached by the little stone bridge over the moat, it has changed very little since the picture was taken, although admission now costs more than six (old) pence!

very clearly, with the remarkable long gallery on the top floor which interrupts the flow of the roof. Although most of the black-and white pattern is a feature of the timber structure, the trefoil pattern on the curved coves under the eaves is only painted onto the plaster. Photograph 48670 shows that it was not there in 1902. The hall looks very much like this today.

Four miles east of Little Moreton, and across the border in Staffordshire, are the ruins of Biddulph Old Hall (42167, page 72-73). During the Civil War the hall withstood a long siege, which only ended when the Parliamentary attackers arrived with a huge gun. The impact of its shot so shook the hall that the defenders surrendered. Members of the Brereton family fought with both the defenders and attackers. Later a small house was built into the ruins. They are private, and visiting is not permitted because the structure is unsafe.

Less than a mile from Biddulph Old Hall stands Biddulph Grange (48669, page 76). In spite of its classical appearance, this mansion was built in the 1890s for a local industrialist, after an earlier house was destroyed by fire. It later became a hospital and has now been converted to residential use. However, its chief point of interest is its remarkable gardens which, surprisingly, largely survived the hospital period and have now been restored and opened to the public by the National Trust.

The boundary between Cheshire and Staffordshire runs along the top of a ridge to the south of Congleton, topped at a prominent point by Mow Cop Castle. This now teeters on the brink of a quarry, although it has been rescued and repaired by the National Trust. The 'castle' is a folly built to improve the view from Rode Hall which stands in the plain below. The Baker-Wilbraham family residing

Passing through the gatehouse passage into the courtyard, we are faced with the hall entrance and the magnificent bay windows. Little has changed here since the photograph was taken - and for centuries before except that, as on the gatehouse, the painted quatrefoils have been removed from the curved coving.

CONGLETON'S COUNTRYSIDE

at Rode Hall have a long-standing connection with Congleton as former hereditary High Stewards of the town. This purely ceremonial post disappeared in the local Government reforms of the 1970s.

Mow Cop holds a prominent place in the history of the Primitive Methodist movement, being the site of some of its early meetings.

The people of Congleton have always had an affection for their local 'mountain', The Cloud (see pages 76-77), which in fact is only just over 1000 ft high. Its heather-covered top was always a popular walk from the town, even before it was acquired by the National Trust in the 1930s. It is an old tradition for Congleton people to climb The Cloud for a dawn service on Easter Day. It can be seen from most places in the town, and the notch in its side gives it an unmistakeable outline. The notch is in fact a large quarry, where stone was collected and transported on a tramway to the nearest road. Much of the stone was used for bridges and buildings and the strengthening of the banks of the Macclesfield canal, which runs near the foot of The Cloud.

Beyond the valley of the Dane, on the western fringe of the Peak District, stands a tall concrete telecommunications tower, still known to local people as the 'Post Office Tower' (C151094, page 78). It stands on Croker Hill, the first ridge of the Pennines. The tower is a prominent landmark in the view from Congleton, and its size can be judged from the apparently tiny buildings near its foot. At this time, the structure of the tower was complete but its equipment had not yet been installed. At first this consisted of huge square-section horns, reminiscent of the gramophone horn in the HMV trademark. These have now been replaced, however, by the more familiar round dishes.

Down on the Cheshire plain, six miles north-west of Congleton, stands the Lovell Radio Telescope at Jodrell Bank (C151092, pages 78-79). It is 250 ft in diameter, and was almost new when this picture was taken. It can be swivelled in any direction, but takes the position shown here when maintenance is in progress. It is accompanied now by several smaller radio telescopes.

BIDDULPH OLD HALL
1898 42167

This romantic prospect of
the ancient structure must
have appealed to the photographer's artistic instincts.

73

BIDDULPH OLD HALL 1902 48667

Here we see the ruins again, this time from a different angle.

CONGLETON'S COUNTRYSIDE

ABOVE: BIDDULPH GRANGE 1902 48669

This view shows the Victorian mansion and one of the more conventional parts of its fascinating gardens.

BELOW MIDDLE: THE CLOUD AND TIMBERSBROOK C1950 C151002

The houses shown here are part of the tiny village of Timbersbrook. The chimney belongs to the Silver Springs Dye works, established here because of the purity of the water. The works are hidden in a little valley. There is now no trace of them, the site being occupied by a car park and picnic tables. Only the mill pond across the road remains.

RIGHT: THE CLOUD FROM BOSLEY C1950 C151001

This view of The Cloud is included here mainly because of the magnificent telephone pole in the foreground. We have almost forgotten these elaborate posts and wires, and the tunes they played in the wind.

MOW COP 1898 42173

The sham castle on Mow Cop is clea visible from much of Congleton.

THE CLOUD FROM BUGLAWTON C1950 C151005

This picture clearly shows the notch in the outline of The Cloud,
which was formed as the result of 19th-century quarrying.

CONGLETON'S COUNTRYSIDE

Above and Below: The GPO Tower c1965 C151094

Right: The Jodrell Bank Radio Telescope c1965 C151092

THE DANE VALLEY

ABOVE: COLLEY MILL BRIDGE c1965 C151102

Congleton lies in the valley of the River Dane - we have already caught a glimpse of the river in the park. Now we move two or three miles upstream to Colley Mill Bridge. This bridge is old and narrow, and was already controlled by traffic lights when this picture was taken. It needed major repairs in the 1980s, but fortunately retained its original form. The traffic lights are still there, as are the attractive cottages, one of which was originally a corn mill.

BELOW LEFT: THE DANE VALLEY 1898 42176

Although not identified by the Frith photographer, this scene appears to be taken near Danebridge, a short way upstream from the weir and canal feeder.

MIDDLE: BOSLEY
RESERVOIR c1965
C151095

A view of the reservoir taken from beside the Buxton Road, looking westwards.

DANE VALLEY BRIDGE 1898 42175

The bridge crosses the feeder channel which carries water from the
Dane to Rudyard Lake.

LEFT: DANE VALLEY WEIR 1898 42177

The Trent and Mersey Canal Company's weir at Gig Hall. The
stepped structure on the left is a fish ladder.

THE DANE VALLEY

BELOW LEFT: BOSLEY RESERVOIR C1965 C151096

This picture was probably taken from the same spot as C151095 on page 80, only the photographer has now turned further southwards to include The Cloud in the background on the right.

BELOW RIGHT: THE RIVER DANE C1960 C151066

This view of the river was not identified by the photographer, but it appears to have been taken from Radnor Bridge.

THE DANE VALLEY

RADNOR BANK ROAD c1960 C151062

This is the road which runs down to Radnor Bridge.

The River Dane, which flows through Congleton, rises on the moors of the Peak District a few miles to the east. It is said to be one of the fastest rising rivers in the country, rain in the hills quickly turning its clear water a peaty brown. Bridges are few: the first upstream from Congleton is the one at Havannah, which serves only the village and mills and has never been a through route for vehicles; the next is Colley Mill bridge where the Buxton road crosses the river.

Further upstream, the Dane passes Bosley and enters a narrow valley in the foothills of the Pennines. A mile or two up this valley at Gig Hall, the Trent and Mersey Canal Company built a large weir (42177, page 81). From this weir they constructed a feeder channel, shown in picture 42175 (page 81). It is built like a miniature canal, with a pathway at one side. For a couple of miles it runs parallel to the river, and has a very gentle gradient so that the river soon runs well below it. When the river leaves the hills and flows northwards towards Bosley and Congleton, the feeder channel turns southwards and crosses the low watershed at Rushton Spencer. It then flows into Rudyard Lake, a major reservoir supplying the Trent and Mersey canal via its Leek branch. Thus water is taken from the Dane (a river which flows into the Weaver and thence into the Irish sea), and diverted into the reservoir whose overflow runs eventually into the Trent and onward into the North Sea.

Photographs C151095 (page 80) and C151096 (Page 82) show Bosley Reservoir, which lies nearly five miles north-east of the town. Situated alongside the Buxton road at the point where it starts to climb into the Pennines, the reservoir was built around 1830 to provide water to the Macclesfield Canal. A feeder channel runs from it to join the canal above the top lock. One interesting feature is the water channel, which runs between the hedges that can be seen in the foreground of C151095 (page 80). It intercepts the water from a side stream and carries it past the reservoir. This probably came about when a miller, further downstream, insisted that his water rights were protected.

Below Congleton the Dane runs through pleasant pastoral countryside before joining the Weaver at Northwich. Radnor Bridge, reached by a narrow twisting side road, is two miles downstream from the town. There is no other road bridge before Holmes Chapel.

TAILPIECE

Congleton people have always been proud of their history, both the period illustrated in this book and of earlier times. A museum displaying the history of the town was opened in 2002. The Museum Trust has also published a book, 'Congleton in the year 2000', which gives a 'snapshot in words' of the town, matching the portrait produced in pictures by the Frith company a century earlier.

But how true, and how complete, a picture of the town did Frith's photographers really present? At the time when they first visited Congleton, there was massive unemployment because of the decline in the silk industry. One result of this was the introduction of the trade of 'fustian cutting', in which the looped pile of a material somewhat like corduroy was slit with a knife to produce a velvet-like fabric. This involved the worker walking the entire length of the mill, slitting one row of loops in a stretched-out piece of material with a special knife, and then walking back again, slitting the next row. It is said that a worker walked over 20 miles on a shift, and bending over the work led to a permanent stoop.

Victorian photographers, including Francis Frith, showed nothing of this, and probably knew nothing of it. They were not social reformers, and most were trying to take photographs that would readily sell. But, nowadays, we do take an interest in these near-forgotten occupations. Only one or two fuzzy pictures of fustian-cutting in Congleton are known: what a pity that the trade was not properly documented on glass plates!

And what of the changes of the first half of the 20th century? The Frith photographers did record some of the more prominent signs of progress - the radio telescope, the telecommunications tower, the bypass, and of course the changing state of the main shopping streets. They showed, too, the outdoor swimming pool, and the hospital, built between the wars, which epitomised the revolution in medicine which so greatly improved the health of the people.

But they missed some of the features that significantly affected the lives of Congleton people. As a result, this book does not show the modern housing estates which were rapidly replacing the run-down Victorian terrace houses, nor the factories that were replacing many of the old mills. Nor does it show our schools, our sports fields, or our theatre. And in particular, there is no general view of the town to show the disappearance of all the mill chimneys, and with them the permanent cloud of smoke that blighted the town in the days when steam was the predominant source of power.

If Francis Frith was to return today, what would we want him to record for posterity? Of course, we would wish for many of the views which his staff did photograph in the late 19th and 20th centuries - the town hall, the park, the churches and inns, the shopping streets, and the attractions of the surrounding countryside. But would we not want him to record, also, those things that touch our lives more deeply? Housing, for example, and industry, and the buildings and the processes that go on within them; sports and other entertainments; the modern equipment of our hospitals and schools; the comfortable homes for old people; the relentless rise in road traffic, the car parked outside nearly every home; the TV supper? Perhaps, even, Manchester airport, to symbolise the foreign holidays that so many of us can now afford?

It would be good if Francis Frith could come back to our town today with his camera.

CONGLETON PARK, THE BOATS c1965 C151043

 This beautiful photograph of the boats in Congleton Park seems a fitting conclusion to this account of the work of the Frith company in and around the town.

NAMES OF PRE-PUBLICATION BUYERS

The following people have kindly supported this book by purchasing limited edition copies prior to publication.

Jean & Geoff Allen of Congleton
Mr P Armitt & Mrs A Armitt and Family
Mr G H Bath & memories of Mrs C J Bath
Mr R A Bath and Family
Mr & Mrs W Beech & Family
Mr Allan Biddulph, Congleton
Mr C & Mrs M Blackshaw & Family
The Boon Family, Congleton
Michael Boon and the Boon Family, Congleton
To Julie, Graham, Ellen & Jayne Booth
Grace Mary Briddock Bradbury
Mr K R & Mrs A M Bradbury and Family
Mr N Brookes, Congleton
To our Daddy, Adrian Brown, love Lydia & Abigail
Margaret & David Brown
Mr S J & Mrs E A Buxton, Congleton
Julian Calvert
Dave, Helen & Molly Cooper, Congleton
Andrea Copeland, Congleton
The Cranney Family of Havannah
Dr J E & Mrs M E Doe, Congleton
The Dowell family, Park Lane, Congleton
Pauline & Richard Drew
Arthur & Madge Gilman,
   Happy 45th Wedding Anniversary
To Richard, Happy Christmas 2005 from your wife,
   Jean Goodall
The Goodier Family, Mossley
Dari Goodwin on her retirement August 2005
Stephen Hadgett, Woodsetton, Dudley
To George & Agnes Hagston of Congleton
Thomas Joseph Hatton, 26th April 2005
The Hey Family - In memory of Audrey
The Hibbert Family, Past and Present
To Steve Hodgkinson on your birthday
Mr B G & Mrs D J Holding, Congleton
To The Holland Family in Australia
Mary Holland, Congleton
In memory of my son Chris, Mary Horne
Gary Marcus Imber, Congleton
Mr Gerry & Mrs Shirley Jarvis
Karen Louise Briddock Jones

Dione Jones, Martin Lancaster, Congleton
Mrs J Laidlaw, Manley, New Zealand
Robert Leith & Family, 'Present and Past'
The Lomas Family, Congleton
The Looker Family, Congleton
The Machin Family, Congleton
Helen & Alexander Moore, Congleton
Mr A & Mrs P Norbury, Congleton
Mr Gary Van Oss, Congleton
Professor David & Mrs Doreen Parsons
To Irene & Chris Proudlove
Mrs M Reddish
Happy Birthday Ruth, 4/9/2005, Mum & Dad
The Zeta Skeet Collective, Congleton
The Spendilow Family
Isabel Mary & Ron Stanley
Mr P & Mrs C Staton, Congleton
Mr J F Stevens, In memory of Lizzie, Jack Stevens,
   Congleton
George Anthony Taylor, Congleton
John & Iris Timmis, Congleton
David Tomlinson, Congleton
In memory of John Moreton Tompson
Linda Tonge, Congleton
Andrew J Torr, Hulme Walfield, Congleton
Roy Turner, Green Acres Farm, Congleton
J A Watson, Congleton
Trevor J Webb for Father's Day
Mr R J & Mrs Y Wharfe and Family, Congleton
The White Family, Congleton
Mr R H Williamson, Congleton
To Joyce Woods on her 50th Birthday
Mr Peter Woods, Congleton
David John Worlock, Congleton
The Worrall Family, Congleton
Mr C & Mrs K L Wright, Congleton
To Karen Wright, love from Mum & Dad
Peter & Sylvia Wright, Congleton
To Stephen Wright, love from Mum & Dad
Jim & Mary Yates, Congleton

INDEX

FRANCIS FRITH'S
TOWN&CITY
MEMORIES

The Francis Frith Collection Titles

www.francisfrith.co.uk

The Francis Frith Collection publishes over 100 new titles each year. A selection of those currently available is listed below. For latest catalogue please contact The Francis Frith Collection. **Town Books** 96 pages, approximately 75 photos. **County and Themed Books** 128 pages, approximately 135 photos (unless specified). All titles hardback with laminated case and jacket, except those indicated pb (paperback)

Accrington Old and New
Alderley Edge and Wilmslow
Amersham, Chesham and Rickmansworth
Andover
Around Abergavenny
Around Alton
Aylesbury
Barnstaple
Bedford
Bedfordshire
Berkshire Living Memories
Berkshire PA
Blackpool Pocket Album
Bognor Regis
Bournemouth
Bradford
Bridgend
Bridport
Brighton and Hove
Bristol
Buckinghamshire
Calne Living Memories
Camberley PA
Canterbury Cathedral
Cardiff Old and New
Chatham and the Medway Towns
Chelmsford
Chepstow Then and Now
Cheshire
Cheshire Living Memories
Chester
Chesterfield
Chigwell
Christchurch
Churches of East Cornwall
Clevedon
Clitheroe
Corby Living Memories
Cornish Coast
Cornwall Living Memories
Cotswold Living Memories
Cotswold Pocket Album
Coulsdon, Chipstead and Woodmanstern
County Durham
Cromer, Sheringham and Holt
Dartmoor Pocket Album
Derby
Derbyshire
Derbyshire Living Memories
Devon
Devon Churches
Dorchester

Dorset Coast PA
Dorset Living Memories
Dorset Villages
Down the Dart
Down the Severn
Down the Thames
Dunmow, Thaxted and Finchingfield
Durham
East Anglia PA
East Devon
East Grinstead
Edinburgh
Ely and The Fens
Essex PA
Essex Second Selection
Essex: The London Boroughs
Exeter
Exmoor
Falmouth
Farnborough, Fleet and Aldershot
Folkestone
Frome
Furness and Cartmel Peninsulas
Glamorgan
Glasgow
Glastonbury
Gloucester
Gloucestershire
Greater Manchester
Guildford
Hailsham
Hampshire
Harrogate
Hastings and Bexhill
Haywards Heath Living Memories
Heads of the Valleys
Heart of Lancashire PA
Helston
Herefordshire
Horsham
Humberside PA
Huntingdon, St Neots and St Ives
Hythe, Romney Marsh and Ashford
Ilfracombe
Ipswich PA
Isle of Wight
Isle of Wight Living Memories
King's Lynn
Kingston upon Thames
Lake District PA
Lancashire Living Memories
Lancashire Villages

Available from your local bookshop or from the publisher

The Francis Frith Collection Titles (continued)

Lancaster, Morecombe and Heysham Pocket Album
Leeds PA
Leicester
Leicestershire
Lincolnshire Living Memoires
Lincolnshire Pocket Album
Liverpool and Merseyside
London PA
Ludlow
Maidenhead
Maidstone
Malmesbury
Manchester PA
Marlborough
Matlock
Merseyside Living Memories
Nantwich and Crewe
New Forest
Newbury Living Memories
Newquay to St Ives
North Devon Living Memories
North London
North Wales
North Yorkshire
Northamptonshire
Northumberland
Northwich
Nottingham
Nottinghamshire PA
Oakham
Odiham Then and Now
Oxford Pocket Album
Oxfordshire
Padstow
Pembrokeshire
Penzance
Petersfield Then and Now
Plymouth
Poole and Sandbanks
Preston PA
Ramsgate Old and New
Reading Pocket Album
Redditch Living Memories
Redhill to Reigate
Rhondda Valley Living Mems
Richmond
Ringwood
Rochdale
Romford PA
Salisbury PA
Scotland
Scottish Castles
Sevenoaks and Tonbridge
Sheffield and South Yorkshire PA
Shropshire
Somerset
South Devon Coast
South Devon Living Memories
South East London
Southampton PA
Southend PA

Southport
Southwold to Aldeburgh
Stourbridge Living Memories
Stratford upon Avon
Stroud
Suffolk
Suffolk PA
Surrey Living Memories
Sussex
Sutton
Swanage and Purbeck
Swansea Pocket Album
Swindon Living Memories
Taunton
Teignmouth
Tenby and Saundersfoot
Tiverton
Torbay
Truro
Uppingham
Villages of Kent
Villages of Surrey
Villages of Sussex PA
Wakefield and the Five Towns Living Memories
Warrington
Warwick
Warwickshire PA
Wellingborough Living Memories
Wells
Welsh Castles
West Midlands PA
West Wiltshire Towns
West Yorkshire
Weston-super-Mare
Weymouth
Widnes and Runcorn
Wiltshire Churches
Wiltshire Living memories
Wiltshire PA
Wimborne
Winchester PA
Windermere
Windsor
Wirral
Wokingham and Bracknell
Woodbridge
Worcester
Worcestershire
Worcestershire Living Memories
Wyre Forest
York PA
Yorkshire
Yorkshire Coastal Memories
Yorkshire Dales
Yorkshire Revisited

See Frith books on the internet at www.francisfrith.co.uk

FRITH PRODUCTS & SERVICES

Francis Frith would doubtless be pleased to know that the pioneering publishing venture he started in 1860 still continues today. Over a hundred and forty years later, The Francis Frith Collection continues in the same innovative tradition and is now one of the foremost publishers of vintage photographs in the world. Some of the current activities include:

Interior Decoration

Today Frith's photographs can be seen framed and as giant wall murals in thousands of pubs, restaurants, hotels, banks, retail stores and other public buildings throughout the country. In every case they enhance the unique local atmosphere of the places they depict and provide reminders of gentler days in an increasingly busy and frenetic world.

Product Promotions

Frith products are used by many major companies to promote the sales of their own products or to reinforce their own history and heritage. Frith promotions have been used by Hovis bread, Courage beers, Scots Porage Oats, Colman's mustard, Cadbury's foods, Mellow Birds coffee, Dunhill pipe tobacco, Guinness, and Bulmer's Cider.

Genealogy and Family History

As the interest in family history and roots grows world-wide, more and more people are turning to Frith's photographs of Great Britain for images of the towns, villages and streets where their ancestors lived; and, of course, photographs of the churches and chapels where their ancestors were christened, married and buried are an essential part of every genealogy tree and family album.

Frith Products

All Frith photographs are available Framed or just as Mounted Prints and Posters (size 23 x 16 inches). These may be ordered from the address below. From time to time other products - Address Books, Calendars, Table Mats, etc - are available.

The Internet

Already ninety thousand Frith photographs can be viewed and purchased on the internet through the Frith websites and a myriad of partner sites.

For more detailed information on Frith companies and products, look at these sites:

www.francisfrith.co.uk
www.francisfrith.com
(for North American visitors)

See the complete list of Frith Books at:

www.francisfrith.co.uk

This web site is regularly updated with the latest list of publications from The Francis Frith Collection. If you wish to buy books relating to another part of the country that your local bookshop does not stock, you may purchase on-line.

For further information, trade, or author enquiries please contact us at the address below:
The Francis Frith Collection, Frith's Barn, Teffont, Salisbury, Wiltshire, England SP3 5QP.
Tel: +44 (0)1722 716 376 Fax: +44 (0)1722 716 881   Email: sales@francisfrith.co.uk

See Frith books on the internet at www.francisfrith.co.uk

FREE PRINT OF YOUR CHOICE

Mounted Print
Overall size 14 x 11 inches (355 x 280mm)

Choose any Frith photograph in this book.
Simply complete the Voucher opposite and
return it with your remittance for £2.25 (to cover
postage and handling) and we will print the
photograph of your choice in SEPIA (size 11 x
8 inches) and supply it in a cream mount with a
burgundy rule line (overall size 14 x 11 inches).
**Please note: photographs with a reference
number starting with a "Z" are not Frith
photographs and cannot be supplied under
this offer.**
Offer valid for delivery to one UK address only.

**PLUS: Order additional Mounted Prints
at HALF PRICE - £7.49 each** (normally £14.99)
If you would like to order more Frith prints from
this book, possibly as gifts for friends and family,
you can buy them at half price (with no
additional postage and handling costs).

PLUS: Have your Mounted Prints framed
For an extra £14.95 per print you can have your
mounted print(s) framed in an elegant pol-
ished wood and gilt moulding, overall size 16 x
13 inches (no additional postage and handling
required).

IMPORTANT!

**These special prices are only available if you use
this form to order . You must use the ORIGINAL
VOUCHER on this page (no copies permitted). We
can only despatch to one UK address. This offer
cannot be combined with any other offer.**

Send completed Voucher form to:
**The Francis Frith Collection, Frith's Barn,
Teffont, Salisbury, Wiltshire SP3 5QP**

CHOOSE A PHOTOGRAPH FROM THIS BOOK

Voucher for **FREE** *and Reduced Price Frith Prints*

*Please do not photocopy this voucher. Only the original is valid,
so please fill it in, cut it out and return it to us with your order.*

Picture ref no	Page no	Qty	Mounted @ £7.49	Framed + £14.95	Total Cost £
		1	Free of charge*	£	£
			£7.49	£	£
			£7.49	£	£
			£7.49	£	£
			£7.49	£	£
			£7.49	£	£

Please allow 28 days for delivery. Offer available to one UK address only

* Post & handling	£2.25
Total Order Cost	£

Title of this book . . . .

I enclose a cheque/postal order for £ . . . .
made payable to 'The Francis Frith Collection'

OR please debit my Mastercard / Visa / Maestro / Amex
card, details below

Card Number

Issue No (Maestro only)   Valid from (Maestro)

Expires   Signature

Name Mr/Mrs/Ms . . . .
Address . . . .
. . . .
. . . .
. . . . Postcode . . . .
Daytime Tel No . . . .
Email . . . .

ISBN 1-85937-977-X   Valid to 31/12/08

Would you like to find out more about Francis Frith?

We have recently recruited some entertaining speakers who are happy to visit local groups, clubs and societies to give an illustrated talk documenting Frith's travels and photographs. If you are a member of such a group and are interested in hosting a presentation, we would love to hear from you.

Our speakers bring with them a small selection of our local town and county books, together with sample prints. They are happy to take orders. A small proportion of the order value is donated to the group who have hosted the presentation. The talks are therefore an excellent way of fundraising for small groups and societies.

Can you help us with information about any of the Frith photographs in this book?

We are gradually compiling an historical record for each of the photographs in the Frith archive. It is always fascinating to find out the names of the people shown in the pictures, as well as insights into the shops, buildings and other features depicted.

If you recognize anyone in the photographs in this book, or if you have information not already included in the author's caption, do let us know. We would love to hear from you, and will try to publish it in future books or articles.

Our production team

Frith books are produced by a small dedicated team at offices in the converted Grade II listed 18th-century barn at Teffont near Salisbury, illustrated above. Most have worked with the Frith Collection for many years. All have in common one quality: they have a passion for the Frith Collection. The team is constantly expanding, but currently includes:

Paul Baron, Jason Buck, John Buck, Ruth Butler, Heather Crisp, David Davies, Louis du Mont, Isobel Hall, Lucy Hart, Julian Hight, Peter Horne, James Kinnear, Karen Kinnear, Tina Leary, Stuart Login, Sue Molloy, Glenda Morgan, Wayne Morgan, Sarah Roberts, Kate Rotondetto, Dean Scource, Eliza Sackett, Terence Sackett, Sandra Sampson, Adrian Sanders, Sandra Sanger, Julia Skinner, Miles Smith, Lewis Taylor, Shelley Tolcher, Lorraine Tuck, Miranda Tunniclisse, David Turner and Ricky Williams.